The Yellow Waters Experience

by

Peter Cook

THE YELLOW WATERS EXPERIENCE

Introduction.

The Australian continent, before it became the land we know today, had to undergo a tremendous upheaval and period of creation, all of which took place long before man, back in the dawn of the planet's history.

In the Top End, an ancient sea bed was pushed upward to form a plateau of 250-300 metres high, worn and hewn by the rugged force of nature to produce an escarpment 500 kms long. Rivers thundered over this vast escarpment in a series of spectacular waterfalls, flowing on through relatively flat expanses, leaving behind an eroding plateau stretching to the sea.

The silt brought down by these rivers, spread over the vast plains causing levy banks to form, which effectively prevented the tidal salt water from entering the plains. These same levies held back the vast quantities of fresh water creating an ideal environment for plant, animal and bird life to flourish.

The Top End of Australia was the 'beach head" or landing spot for the first people -the Aborigines - to set foot on this great continent. They landed literally into a place of milk and honey. Birds, fish, crocodiles, turtles, snakes and animals abounded in and around the prolific billabongs that dotted the north. These animals made life comparatively easy for these skilled black hunters.

It didn't take these inhabitants long to discover that many of the trees and shrubs produced edible fruits and berries, and that various sections of the plants could be used to manufacture a wide range of products, such as baskets, mats, fish traps, spears and even medicines. In fact so rich were the pickings that these new people rapidly multiplied and spread over the entire continent. Australia would have been a wonderful place to live in those early years, life would have been sweet.

The early 17th century saw the first Europeans arrive in this southern land. The Maccassans, like the Aborigines, also came to Australia from the north, hoping to find a new life in a new land. Fortunately they were able to live in relatively peaceful co-existence with their black neighbors, although they never really settled, choosing instead to sail down from the Indonesian Archipelago each wet season and return again each dry. The strong monsoon winds powering their praus.

In 1644 Abel Tasman sailed around the Top End and and named a section "Arnham Land", after his vessel, the Arnham. The coastline still bears the name although the spelling has been changed to Arnhem Land. In 1818, Captain King sailed the same section of coastline as Tasman and proceeded unimaginatively to name the South, East and West Alligator Rivers after the large reptiles he spotted basking on the beaches. He was wrong of course, the saurians were not alligators at all, but salt water crocodiles.

Unlike the Aboriginal people, the early settlers were not prepared to live off the land, to let nature feed them, they wanted to till the land and farm it. Before long they had introduced new animals to the continent, such as horses, cattle, deer, and pigs. Fifty Asian water buffalo arrived from Timor in 1824. And in the same year gold was discovered and claims were staked fast and furious, with the Chinese flocking to the goldfields. But the land was rugged and hard to tame, the weather was hot and unrelenting and as a result many of the miners and settlers were forced to abandon the north and find an easier place to live.

As the settlers and soldiers abandoned their forts, the horses, buffalo, deer, cattle and pigs were released into the wild. Most found an abundance of wild "tucker" on the prolific wetlands and forested areas of the north. Their numbers boomed, in particular the buffalo and pigs. Unfortunately local Aboriginal

clans were "traditionally" greatly affected by these events and the environment suffered considerable damage from the introduced animals.

The mid to late 1800's proved a very important time of discovery for the early explorers traversing the continent. Many of the plants, birds, animals, rivers and prominent land marks were named by men such as Ludwig Leichhardt. It soon became apparent to many folks that the "Top End" was home to a wide variety and abundance of flora and fauna. It also proved scenically breathtaking in rugged beauty, as well as containing a wealth of cultural significance, with much of the environment and Aboriginal art sites extremely fragile. They soon realised that unless something was done, much of this heritage could be lost to the nation.

In April 1979, 6144 sq kms of land within the Alligator Rivers area was designated a National Park and named "Kakadu", which incidentally is a mispronunciation of the word "Gagadju", which literally means "Land of the People". In August of that same year Kakadu was added to the World Heritage List, the highest status that can be given to a National Park. Kakadu was recognised as an internationally important wetland area for wildlife. It was the first Australian National Park to receive the World Heritage status.

In February 1984, stage two was added, a further 6,929 sq kms of land came under World Heritage listing. In that same year a buffalo eradication program was launched to eliminate the great grey beasts from within the park borders. Unfortunately the great lumbering beasts were responsible for huge damage to wetlands of the park.

But Kakadu seemed to have an insatiable appetite for land and in 1987 another 6,726 sq kms of land was added to stages one and two, increasing the overall size of the park to a mammoth 19,799 sq kms. This makes the park one tenth of the size of the state of Victoria!

The addition of Stage 3 means that Kakadu is now unique among Australian National Parks in three ways......

1. It was the first Australian National Park to receive World Heritage status.

2. It is Australia's largest National Park.

3. It contains a complete river system within its boundaries. (The river the South Alligator, is also Kakadu's largest).

Kakadu has six topographical regions within its boundaries, the major region being the tidal flats, flood plains, lowlands, escarpment and plateaus. Such a diverse range of habitats means that it is home to some 280 species of birds (about one third of the total specimens in Australia can be found within Kakadu), 54 species of mammals, 78 species of reptiles, 22 species of amphibians, 45 species of fresh water fish (about 25% of Australia's freshwater fish species), approximately 10,000 species of insects, not including spiders and 900 plant species. Kakadu is indeed a flora and fauna spectacular!

Within the Kakadu boundaries lies the popular, breathtakingly beautiful spot called Yellow Waters. Situated right in the heartland area of the park on the South Alligator River floodplain, it is by far one of the best places to observe Kakadu's abundant flora and fauna wealth. Here within its myriads of waterways I was fortunate enough to spend some 8 months of my life. It was a very enjoyable, peaceful time which I shall treasure for the rest of my life. This book then, is a result of my time spent here and it is dedicated to every person who partakes in the "Yellow Waters experience"....it's one you will never forget!

Pelicans, "Pelecarus consphullatus", are familiar sights at Yellow Waters, strangely enough for such a large bird they are prone to predators. Crocodiles prey upon them and even the white breasted sea eagle attacks them.

<u>Top</u> "Djigarrapa" was the name given to Yellow Waters by the Aboriginal people. A number of tribes used the billabong as a hunting area. Here we have Minnie Alderson, a descendant of the Murrumbur tribe looking for file snakes.
<u>Centre</u> The brolga, one of two Australian cranes. These birds are noted for their mating dances and they mate for life. The brolga is the "bird in the sun" featured in the NT symbol.

Birdlife

Yellow Waters is a bird watchers paradise, in fact some 30 to 50 percent of all bird species in Australia can be viewed around its waterways. At various times of the year the myriads of waterholes and "everglades" are teeming with birdlife, everything from ducks and waterfowl, to eagles and kites. The ceaseless honking of the magpie geese is almost synonymous with the place.

But many more species abound. The rainbow beeeater, kingfishers, snakebirds, cormorants, egrets and pelicans - they are all here.

Kingfishers

The azure kingfisher "Alcedo azurea" is a beautiful bird that graces the waterways of Yellow Waters. It feeds almost exclusively on a fish diet and can be observed going about its busy daily schedule of finding and hunting prey. The colourful little bird can often be observed with its characteristic habit of bobbing its head up and down as its high pitched call floats over the serene billabongs.

Waterbirds

Waterbirds flock to Yellow Waters, indeed they make up one of the areas most popular attractions. Here we have a stately jabiru acting as sentinel over a flock of majestic royal spoonbills "Platalea regia". The spoonbills are interesting to observe and here they are engaged in a feeding frenzy, sweeping their spoon shaped bills through the mud in search of food.

In the background the ever present magpie geese watch on with little interest.

From about September the northern part of Australia sees the first migratory birds from the northern hemisphere such as the sandpiper. Photo here is of the wood sandpiper. These birds remain here in the north until about April when they return to places like Siberia to nest.

Centre Left

If you look closely among the trees lining the edge of the main channels you may be lucky enough to spot a Rufous night heron.

Young night herons have a mottled plumage while the adult bird, such as this one, are a handsome brown.

Bottom

The Ibis is a common bird right throughout the Top End and here we have the strawnecked ibis feeding in the shallows.

When the water in Yellow Waters recede large numbers of wading birds, such as the ibis and herons, move in to feed. This shot is of the handsome pied heron *Ardea pictata*.

Centre right

Another of the ibis family, the sacred ibis.

Above

The elegant looking pied stilt, or black winged stilt, arrives at Yellow Waters during the latter part of the dry season when the water levels have dropped sufficiently to allow wading birds to feed.

Right

The regal looking royal spoonbill "platalea regia" also makes it home here and can be quite numerous, large flocks can often be seen feeding in the shallows.

17

Darter or Snakebird

Another bird that makes its home at Yellow Waters all year round is the Darter, Anhinga or commonly called Snake bird. "Anhinga melanogastei." Related to the cormorant, it is a bird that spends much of its time underwater in search of fish. Using its beak as a spear, the bird is a keen hunter. Like the cormorant family the darter has no waterproofing on its feathers and must spend time drying its plumage in the strong northern sunshine. The bird gains its name from its appearance, the long neck protruding from the water gives a distinct outline of a snake. Males are completely black while the female is much paler with a grey or white front plumage.

Jabirus

The Jabiru is more correctly known as the black necked stork "Ephippioihynchus asiaticus" and is reasonably common throughout the north. A strikingly handsome bird they are Australia's only real stork. Females can be identified by their brillliant yellow eyes, males have black eyes.

The Jabiru builds its nest high in the tops of the wetlands trees.

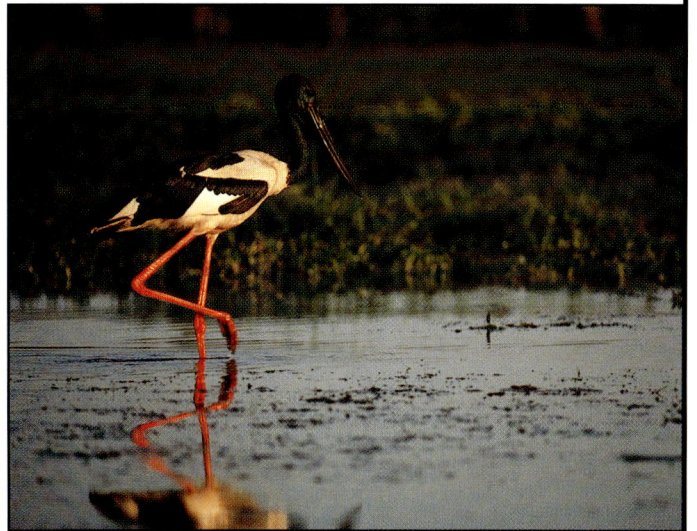

Pelicans

Pelicans are a common sight at Yellow Waters - indeed some years back when the centre of the continent was in the grip of a terrible drought and much of the inland water dried up, thousands of these black and white giants of the sky migrated to this oasis. Many of the birds arrived so weak and undernourished that they died by the hundreds.

Pelicans are wonderful fliers and they can often be observed high overhead riding the wind currents and thermals.

The Majestic Egret

Of all the birds at Yellow Waters the majestic egret is one of the most striking. Large numbers of these birds move into Yellow Waters to take advantage of the abundance of food, feeding in the soft mud and shallow waters, particularly as the waters recede.

Several species of egret can be found here, but by far the most common is the intermediate or plumed egret "Egretta intermedia" (two shots on this page).

The largest egret in Australia, the great egret,"Egretta alba" is also quite common (photo on left hand page).

Sometimes egrets are so prolific in Yellow Waters that they look like giant white water lilies among the beautiful green water plants of the billabong.

The comb creasted Jacana "Irediparra gallinacea" has many names including lotus bird and lilytrotter. The latter is an appropriate name as the bird has the largest feet in proportion to body size of any bird in the world. The large feet enable it to trot across the lilypads and other floating vegetation. It even builds its nest on a lily pad.

Adult Jacanas have a distinctive fleshy comb on their head but the young birds don't and are paler in colour.

Lilytrotter or
Lotus Bird

Corellas

Little Corellas are a common inhabitant of the paperbark trees surrounding Yellow Waters. Looking very much like a sulphur crested cockatoo - which they are often mistaken for - they have been given the nickname of "nature's alarm clock".

Camp under a tree full of corellas and you will see just why they get that name.

Kites, Hawks and Eagles

Whistling kites are the most common bird of prey inhabiting Yellow Waters. Excellent scavengers, tourists are attracted by the bird's ability to snatch food from plates, out of a hand or even catch food thrown into the air. They will even pick up food and fish entrails from the water while still in flight.
(Kites are featured in bottom photo on left and on left hand page).

King of the sky over Yellow Waters and definately the most spectacular of all the birds is the magnificent white breasted sea eagle "Haliaeetus leulogastei". With a wing span of 2 metres the sea eagle is the second largest bird of prey in Australia. Eagles mate for life and form a strong union, they are regularly seen flying and hunting together and their call to each other from their favourite trees is a joy to all who hear it.

(Photos top on left, above and below)

Ducks & Geese

Main Photo

Magpie geese are by far the most numerous birds to visit Yellow Waters, naturally brilliant black and white in colour, many of the birds become stained and discoloured from the muddy waters. Once countless thousands of these birds flapped and honked their way across the Top End but numbers are declining.

Top left

Two species of whistling ducks visit the place, and this one, the plumed or grass whistler is by far the most handsome and common. The duck, as the name suggests is not capable of quacking and makes a whistling noise.

Top right

Another type of duck to visit the place is the Burdekin or radjah smelduck, a handsome duck that is an excellent parent and can often be observed in pairs or with a host of ducklings. This bird is feeding with a pied stilt.

Bottom left

A green pygmy goose "Nettapus pulchellus", which is actually a duck, and makes its home in Yellow Waters all year round. They also mate for life and are usually seen in pairs. A rather timid bird that is difficult to approach.

The rainbow bee-eater "Merops oinatus', must surely be the most beautifully coloured bird at Yellow Waters. They catch insects on the wing with a wonderful display of aerobatics, usually pounding the insect on a tree branch before swallowing it. Common during the wet season the birds move south to nest during the dry.

The Tawny frog mouth takes some spotting as it sits imitating a dead branch.

Right hand page

The little pied cormorant, close relative of the anhinga (snake bird) is a common sight around the water ways. A prolific fish hunter the cormorant makes its permanent home in Yellow Waters.

Left Top

A young rufous night heron.

Centre left

Large numbers of these glossy ibis flock to Yellow Waters to feed in the soft mud left behind as the waters receede.

Bottom left

Gull billed tern in flight.

Top
    A Masked lapwing "Vanellus miles". These birds nest during the dry and chicks, such as this one are able to feed themselves from the time they hatch.

Above
    An adult specimen of the masked lapwing.

Right
    A whiskered tern. These birds hawk insects on the wing as well as plunge into the water in spectacular dives to take small fish.

Centre
    Huge flocks of magpie geese, such as this, are not uncommon at Yellow Waters.

Top
    Another dry season visitor to the Yellow Waters billabong is this black fronted dotterel.

Top

Yellow Waters is home to several species of very secretive and seldom seen birds such as this great billed heron.

Above

Two brolgas feed with a flock of magpie geese, these brolgas are renown for their ability to dance and Aborigines often mimic them in their tribal dancing.

39

Left page
    Willy Wagtails are another common resident of Yellow Waters, the birds nest all year round.

Top and top left
    The abundance of waterbirds at Yellow Waters can be seen by these photos.

Left bottom
    A rufous banded honeyeater "Conophila albogularis".

Flora of Yellow Waters
Lilies

Main Photo
Top End waters can be a scene of great floral beauty, a kaleidoscope of blue, pink, purple and white giant water lilies.

Top Left
The nocturnal pink lily which opens at night and closes during the early part of the day.

Bottom Left
   Blue lily.

Other Photos
   A variety of water lilies that abound in the billabongs of the north.

The Top End blue lily

Leaves of the paperbark, a tree that played a very important role in the daily lives of the Aborigines.

The two main reasons why Yellow Waters received its name are the subject of controversy. Some say it's because of the yellow snow flake lily, as in the photos. These attractive flowers grow over large expanses of water giving it a yellow effect. However these lilies have been noticably absent from Yellow Waters of late and it is more likely the name came from the growth of a yellow algae which is prolific during the dry. The algae which grows in the sheltered parts of the billabong gives the appearance of yellow water.

Left

Paperbarks which are prolific in the area.

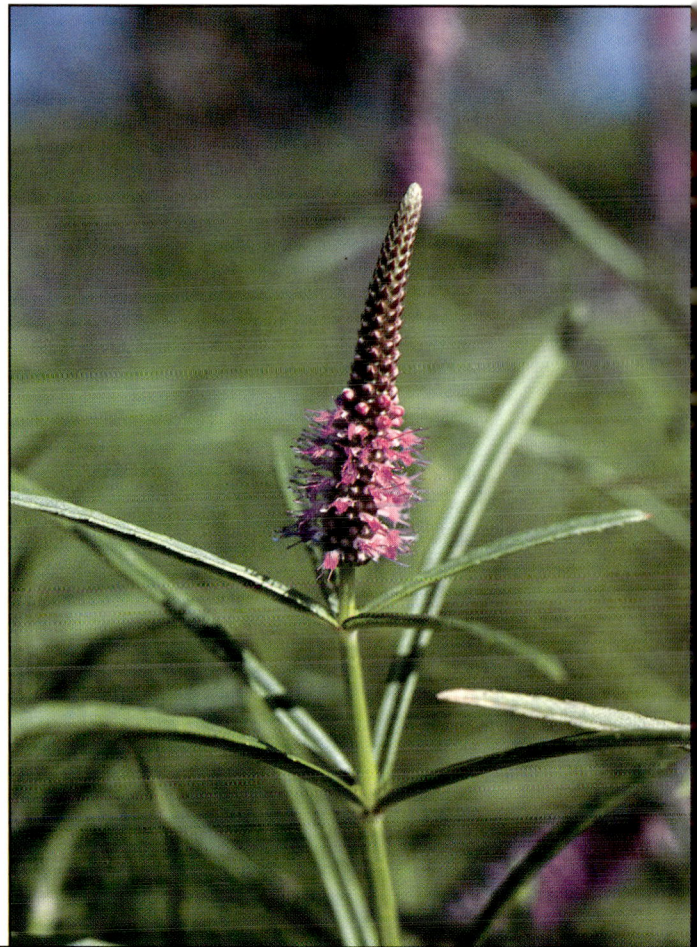

Right hand page
    Fresh water mangrove flowering.

Right
    Patches of native lavendar grow alongside the billabong giving a country garden effect.

Above
    The huge floating water lily leaves make an impressive sight, sometimes covering vast areas of the billabongs and providing an ideal habitat for aquatic life.

The two main waterways that make up Yellow Waters are scenically different. The side branch of the South Alligator River is generally deep and steep sided with trees lining both banks. The main plants are fresh water mangroves, which flower profusely, Arnhem Land bamboo, a native species, pandanus palms and the ever present paperbark trees.

Top Left
Water snowflakes.

Bottom Left
Waterplants on the mirror like surface.

Right
A number of cabbage tree palms grow alongside the main channel, the heart or bulb at the top being edible.

The Jim Jim Creek section of Yellow Waters is basically the complete opposite to the side branch of the South Alligator. It flows through a very open area of flood plain with a few paperbarks growing along the banks. The paperbarks are very abundant in the upper areas of the billabong. The channel generally is quite shallow along the edges and the banks are minimal.

This presents a tremendous feeding area for a rich variety of birdlife, and in fact it is the birdlife that makes Yellow Waters internationally famous.

Yellow Waters is one of the largest permanent water holes in all of Kakadu National Park. As the water levels recede across the Top End, and many of the other wetlands and billabongs dry up, huge numbers of wildlife migrate to this area and the rich feeding it provides.

It can be a veritable "oasis" in the desert.

A prolific growing plant with dark green leaves and a white flower may cover the floodplains with a mat of floating vegetation (photo top far right). Looking somewhat like watercress the plant is "Ludwigia adsenders". Giant waterlilies push through this mat with a rich variety of colour, producing a beautiful floral bloom, a scene that at times can be breathtaking.

Bottom left
Sunset is a very special time at Yellow Waters, with every sunset being different but almost without exception they are breathtakingly beautiful, especially in the dry season.

Bottom right
The occasional tree orchid grows on the paperbarks.

Top right
Another floating mat plant, the morning glory or kangkong grows in profusion during the wet season.

Crocodiles are one of the biggest tourist attractions in the Top End, Yellow Waters being no exception to the rule. The numbers of the big saurians start to increase in the billabong about May, the time they are returning from their nesting. Big specimens inhabit the waterholes and they can frequently be observed basking in the sun, usually early in the morning or late afternoon during the dry season. Nothing is safe from the jaws of a salt water croc. Competition between crocs becomes high towards the end of the dry and fighting over food is not an uncommon sight.

Far right

A croc has a pelican by the neck while a jabiru observes from a safe distance.

One croc has the pelican by the neck while another approaches from the rear. A fight was about to break out.

Crocodiles

The Top End has always been rich in reptile life, Yellow Waters being no exception to that rule. Top right we find a beautifully marked carpet python, quite harmless, while bottom right we find Burtons snake lizard "lialis burtonis".

These waterholes are home to many snakes and lizards but the file snake "Acrochordus aratuae" is one of the most common (top right). Prized for food by the Aborigines, the women who hunted them would bite their heads to break the reptile's neck.

To catch a file snake is quite simple, just enter a crocodile infested billabong, completely submerge yourself under the water and then search among the pandanus roots for the snake. Next pull it out of the roots, pop its head into your mouth, close your teeth, a quick jerk to break the neck and it's all over. The snake gains its name from its roughly textured skin. They are an aquatic snake capable of reaching 2.5 metres in length but are non venomous. Besides collecting file snakes, it was the womens job to hunt turtles, croc, fish, yabbies, mussels and birds.

Goannas

Frogs

The gould's monitor lizard or goanna can often be seen basking in the sun early in the morning, before heading of across the flood plains in search of insects, eggs, fish or other reptiles and carrion.

During the wet season the edges of the main channels are just teeming with green frogs (top photo) "litoria dahli". These little fellows are consumed in huge quantities by the birds and reptiles of the area.

Other species of frogs inhabit the paperbarks as well as the waterholes, these bottom two shots are of "genus litoria"

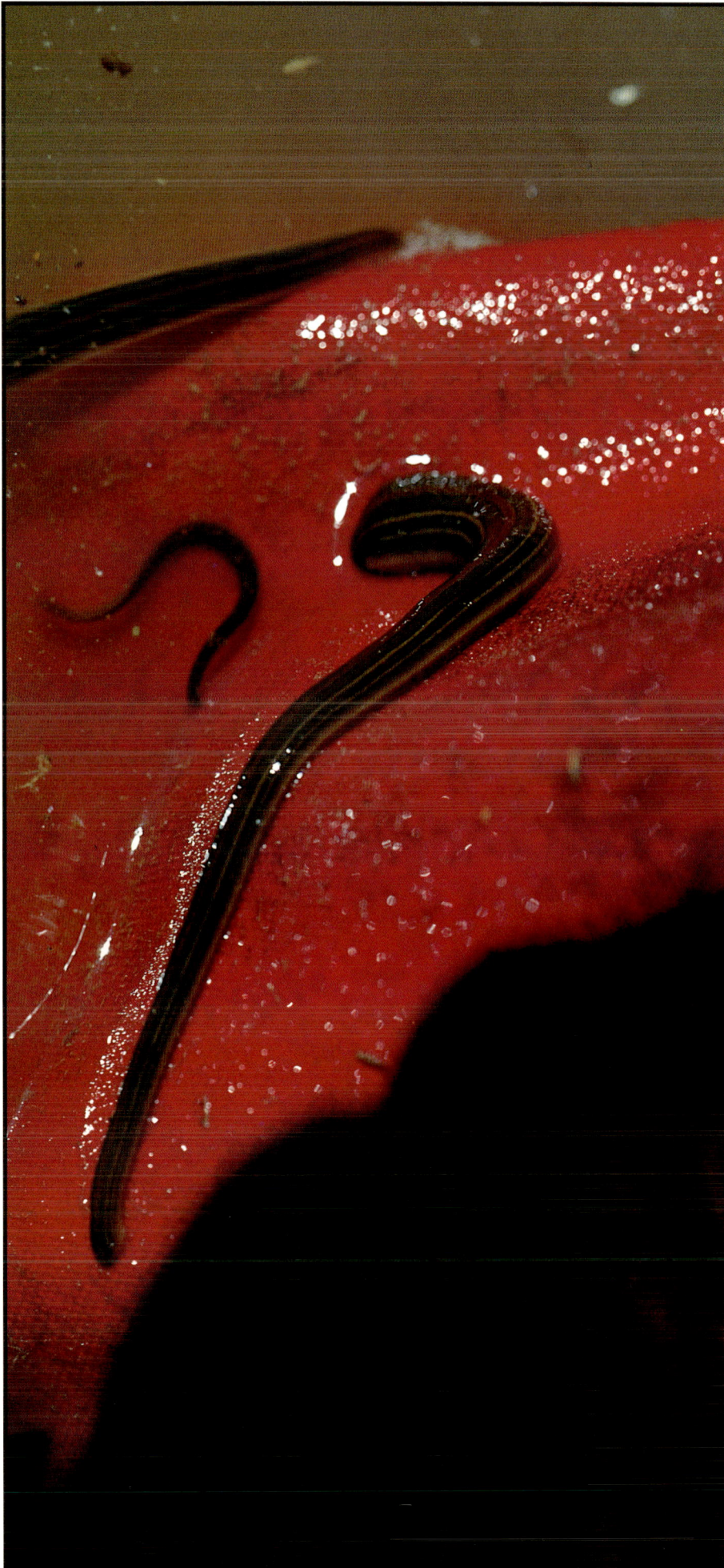

The Yellow Waters area is rich in insect life such as these wonderful and industrious green ants (top right). They build their nests in the trees by fastening leaves together with silk, but be warned they are quick to defend their homes regardless of the size of the intruder.

Even the beetles here have Aboriginal art work on their backs (Far right centre)

Left
Two very good reasons why most people prefer not to swim in Yellow Waters - crocodiles and this little fellow - the leech.

Other creatures to inhabit the place include the Saint Andrews Cross Spider (below) and a variety of grasshoppers.

Insects

Once the rains cease - usually late in March - the water levels start to drop considerably, in fact about three metres. Dry land is exposed to the northern sun and the billabongs become separated again. During this period as the flood plains dry out, a tiny black beetle emerges to consume the green ludwigia plant. (Photo bottom left)

Despite the fact that this is the time the giant water lilies start to die, it is also the time when Yellow Waters really comes alive.

Photo above is one of the many moths that abound on tropical nights.

Of the myriads of insects in the Yellow Waters area, few are more beautiful or spectacular than the dragonflies.

Usually one of the first signs heralding the oncoming dry season is the welcome appearance of these miniature "helicopters".

They come in many shapes and sizes.

Animals

Buffalo were introduced to Australia from Asia by the British Redcoats back in the mid 19th century along with pigs, Timor ponies, banteng cattle and sambar deer.

When the British abandoned their forts along the north coast, they released these animals back into the wild. The deer, ponies and banteng barely held their own and are now restricted to the Coburg Peninsula, however the buffalo and pigs thrived in this environment and have spread right across the Top End.

Indeed Yellow Waters was the main base camp for the buffalo shooters during the heyday of the hunting for their hides.

About 20 years ago Yellow Waters was home to large herds of these lumbering grey beasts and the damage they created is still evident during the dry season when many of the old wallows and hoof prints are exposed.

Buffalo numbers have been greatly reduced, in fact the NT government has a very controversial policy of wiping them out entirely in the wild, but small numbers can still be spotted in the area.

Wild pigs frequent the area also, but due to their nocturnal feeding habits they are seldom seen during the day.

Wild horses, or brumbies, can be observed in small herds grazing among the paperbarks. These animals are not true brumbies but are domesticated stock gone wild, most likely from the buffalo hunting days or nearby cattle stations. Again the Federal Government has come under heavy criticism for its policy in the north of shooting these horses from the air. Outcries from as far afield as Sweden have been voiced over their slaughter.

Sunset is always a beautiful sight to behold here at Yellow Waters. Many tourists can be seen, cameras in hand, as they await the red ball to disappear over the billabongs.

Other creatures of the night that one is likely to encounter are the flying fox or giant fruit bat, Australia's largest bat. This shot shows a tree full of the unusual creatures.

Days are spent hanging upside down like this. However as the sun sets they take to the sky in their thousands in search of nectar or fruit bearing trees.

Agile wallabies "macropus agillius" are a very common macropod that inhabit the paper-bark groves along the billabongs. During the evening and early morning they can be seen in their hundreds feeding on the new grass shoots.

The Seasons
The Wet

Only two seasons are experienced in the tropical north - the wet and the dry. The wet usually runs from November through to March, the dry from May to September - the in between months being transitional. During the five months of the wet about 1.3 metres of rain falls in the area. Much of this is collected within the South Alligator and Jim Jim Creek catchment areas causing the rivers to rise and burst their banks. They spread over the floodplains and turn the area into a vast lake. At times the South and East Alligator Rivers have actually joined in one mighty stretch of water some 70-80 kms wide. The wet is a beautiful time of the year with the sky alive with dramatic and often violent thunderstorms. Giant water lilies grow in profusion while the vegetation takes on a lush green, turning the whole of the north into a veritable Garden of Eden. In fact the new name adopted for the wet is the "green season". During this time many of the plants and trees are submerged under water, however most are adaptable to the north's - flood or fire existence. The paperbark trees are a good example as they have waterproof bark with thousands of tiny air tubes which transmit the air down into the root system.

A spectacular
Yellow
Waters
Electrical
Storm

The Dry

Season

Once the monsoon rains cease in March the water levels in the area start to drop dramatically. The areas surrounding the billabong turn from green to brown. However this is the time Yellow waters comes alive as birds and animals begin to move back to the permanent water. Many species of birds are either returning to Northern Australia or have been nesting.

Sacred, strawnecked and glossy ibis, herons and egrets are just some of the birds that can be observed.

The days are less humid and the nights much cooler during the early part of the dry as atmospheric temperatures drop dramatically. Mist begins to rise from the warm water which explodes into colour as the sun appears in the eastern horizon. Sunrise is often the most pleasant time of the day and makes for a time of spectacular photography.

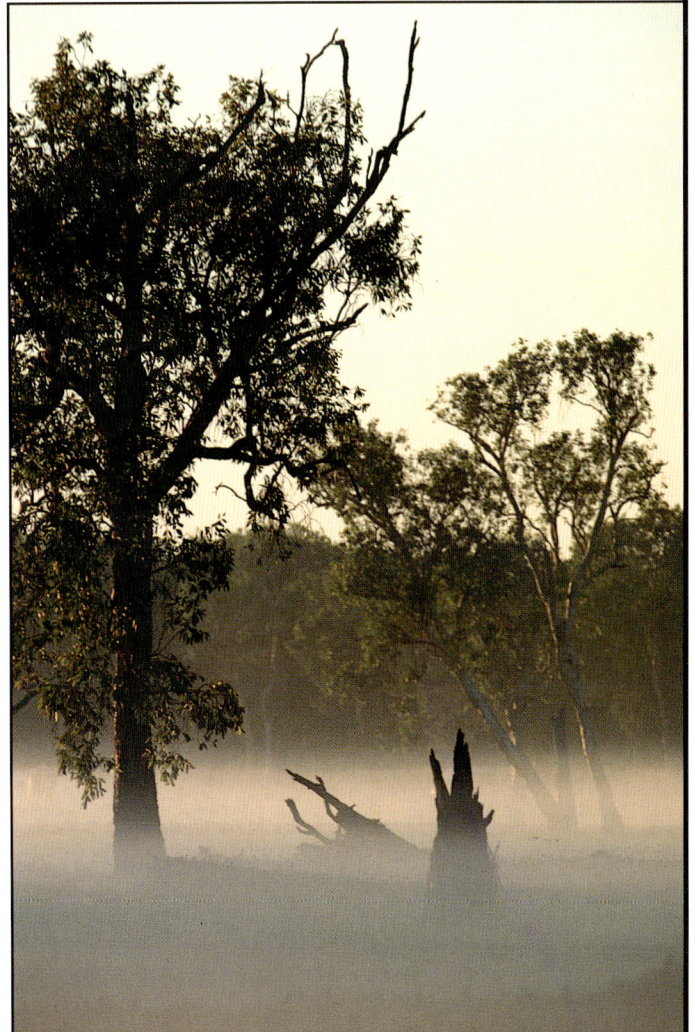

Yellow Waters

Djigarrapa was the name given to the place by the Aboriginal people. A number of tribes used the billabong as a hunting area. It is made up of two major waterways-the Jim Jim Creek and a side branch of the South Alligator River. The Jim Jim channel enter the South Alligator after flowing some 12 km overland and then travels a further 70 km before entering the Arafura Sea. Yellow Waters is approximately 85 kms from the sea. Photo below is of the Gagudju Lodge Cooinda Resort beside Home Billabong.

Yellow Waters is a true billabong in that during the dry season it is a body of water trapped in river beds but does not flow. During the wet, these river courses run normally. Access to Yellow waters can be a problem during the wet season when the roads some-

The Place

imes flood. Access then is by way of boat from
Home Billabong at Cooinda.

Not just for the birdwatchers and tourists, the billabongs here have been favourite fishing places for many years. It is home to the legendary barramundi, tarpon, catfish, long-om, archerfish, sleepy cod and saratoga.

The store at Cooinda was orginally run by Tom and Judy Opitz (a book has been written about their early exploits) in a tin shed on the banks of the Jim Jim. Today the Gagudju Lodge Cooinda Resort is a far cry from those primitive early days. Coaches bring tourists from all over the globe to enjoy this fabulous place and they are able to enjoy it in modern air conditioned comfort.

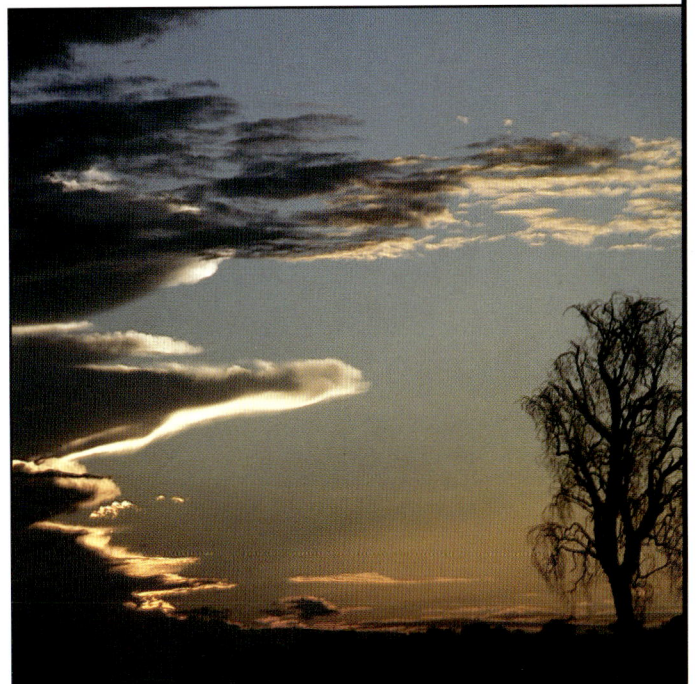

Yellow Waters Boat Cruises

Boat cruises are operated five times a day, every day of the year. Unfortunately it is a very difficult assessment to advise the best time to see the billabong, it is a place that is constantly changing with the seasons, time of day etc. However as a general rule early morning and late afternoon are best, depending of course on what you wish to see.

For lilies and other flowers the wet season from Januray to April, any time of day after they have opened.

For crocodiles the dry season from May to November is best. Early in the dry they tend to remain submerged in the mornings to keep warm, coming out to bask in the sun about midday. As the season progresses and the days get hotter they tend to sun bake early or late in the day, staying in the water during the middle of the day.

For birds late in the dry is best, early mornings and late afternoons. However no matter what time you decide to visit, your stay at Yellow Waters will be an experience you will remember for a life time.